for '01 . . .
You Suckas!

Other books by Aaron McGruder

The Boondocks: Because I Know You Don't Read the Newspaper

Fresh for '01 . . . You Suckas!

A Boondocks™ Collection
by Aaron McGruder

**Andrews McMeel
Publishing**

Kansas City

The Boondocks is distributed internationally by Andrews McMeel Universal.

Fresh for '01 . . . You Suckas copyright © 2001 by Universal Press Syndicate. All rights reserved. Printed in the United States of America. No part of this book may be used or reproduced in any manner whatsoever without written permission except in the case of reprints in the context of reviews. For information write Andrews McMeel Publishing, an Andrews McMeel Universal company, 4520 Main Street, Kansas City, Missouri 64111.

01 02 03 04 05 BAH 10 9 8 7 6 5 4 3 2 1

ISBN: 0-7407-1395-7

Library of Congress Catalog Card Number: 00-108459

The Boondocks may be viewed on the Internet at:
www.boondocks.net

—— **ATTENTION: SCHOOLS AND BUSINESSES** ——

Andrews McMeel books are available at quantity discounts with bulk purchase for educational, business, or sales promotional use. For information, please write to: Special Sales Department, Andrews McMeel Publishing, 4520 Main Street, Kansas City, Missouri 64111.

This book is dedicated as always to
my family, my friends, to my always patient syndicate,
and to everyone who helped me while I was sick
so I could get to this second book.
Thank you.

8

MORE CONTROVERSY SURROUNDING BOB JONES UNIVERSITY TODAY — THE SCHOOL WHOSE BAN ON INTER-RACIAL DATING DREW CRITICISM TO THE BUSH CAMPAIGN WHEN HE SPOKE THERE WEEKS AGO.

TODAY, PRESIDENTIAL HOPEFUL ALAN KEYES WAS BEATEN BY BOB JONES UNIVERSITY SECURITY AS HE ARRIVED TO SPEAK AT THE SCHOOL. IT SEEMS A WHITE FEMALE AIDE WAS MISTAKEN FOR A GIRLFRIEND.

IT WAS MY FAULT. I SHOULD HAVE BEEN MORE CAREFUL! I FEEL MUCH BETTER! REALLY!! END AFFIRMATIVE ACTION!!

KEYES RETURNED TO GIVE HIS SPEECH AFTER AGREEING TO "KEEP HIS DISTANCE FROM THE WHITE WOMEN" AND KEEP "EYEBALLING" TO A MINIMUM.

UNIVERSITY OFFICIALS REFUSED TO APOLOGIZE FOR THE BEATING, SAYING: "HEY, IT LOOKED TO US LIKE HE WAS VIOLATING GOD'S WILL BY DATING A WHITE LADY. BETTER SAFE THAN SORRY."

OK, CLASS, TODAY WE WRAP UP OUR CHAPTER ON GEORGE WASHINGTON CARVER ...

FINALLY!!! THANK YOU ... NO OFFENSE TO GEORGE, BUT DAG ... HOW MANY TIMES DO WE NEED TO HEAR THE SAME PEANUT STORIES?

EVERY BLACK HISTORY MONTH IT'S THE SAME THING — THE UNDERGROUND RAILROAD AND GEORGE WASHINGTON CARVER. LIKE NOTHING ELSE EVER HAPPENED TO BLACK PEOPLE! MAYBE NOW WE CAN LEARN SOMETHING NEW ...

SO PLEASE TURN YOUR BOOKS TO PAGE 35 ...

SOMETHING WE HAVEN'T HEARD ABOUT A THOUSAND TIMES ALREADY ...

AND LET'S LOOK AT MARTIN LUTHER KING JR.

NEVER MIND.

SO WHO'S RUNNING FOR PRESIDENT? IS BILL CLINTON RUNNING?

NO. WHY?

WHY ISN'T HE RUNNING? I WANNA VOTE FOR CLINTON!

SINCE WHEN DO YOU CARE? WHAT DO YOU KNOW ABOUT POLITICS?

MAN, CLINTON IS THE MAN!! HE'S A PLAYA PRESIDENT!! HE'S A PIMP!! WHOEVER ELSE IS RUNNING, THEY AIN'T SMOOTH LIKE MY DAWG CLINTON!

OK, SO YOU DO KNOW SOMETHING ABOUT POLITICS ...

HEY ... YOU THINK I COULD GROW UP TO BE PRESIDENT PIMP LIKE BILL CLINTON?

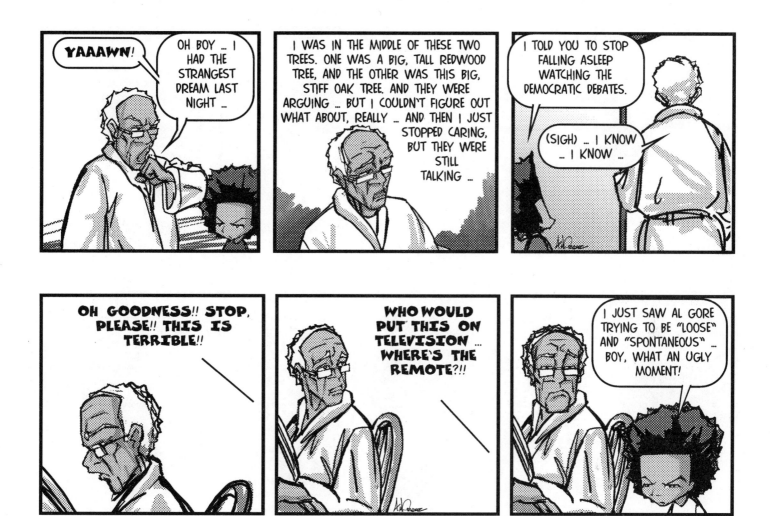

SURE IS A LOT GOING ON IN THE WORLD ... THE PRESIDENTIAL RACE, THE ECONOMY, NEW DISCOVERIES IN MEDICINE AND TECHNOLOGIES ...

HERE'S AN IDEA! INSTEAD OF WATCHING VIDEOS ALL DAY, WHY DON'T YOU WATCH THE NEWS?

WHY?

BECAUSE I KNOW YOU DON'T READ THE NEWSPAPER ...

NO, I MEANT, **WHY** DO YOU THINK I'LL EVER BE A GOOFY NERD LIKE YOU?

WELL, GRANDDAD ... HERE'S WHAT **I** THINK ABOUT THIS WHOLE SOUTH CAROLINA FLAG BUSINESS ...

Editor's Note:
The heavy-handed and not at all balanced political opinions presented in this cartoon may be offensive to some readers. Therefore, we are replacing the remainder of this strip with an earlier installment.

We apologize for any inconvenience ...

(This kid is no Garry Trudeau...)

... NO, IT STANDS FOR **B**LACK **E**XPLOITATION **T**ELEVISION ... **B**UTTS **E**VERY **T**IME ...

Editor's Note:

Oops, we were supposed to ban that one, too ...

HEY HUEY, HAVE YOU SEEN THAT BEER COMMERCIAL WITH THE BLACK GUYS ON THE PHONE AND THEY'RE ALL YELLING —

YES! BUT I HAVE A HEADACHE, SO PLEASE DON'T —

WAAAASSZZUUUUP!!

HELLO? IS THIS HUEY?

YEAH.

WAAASSZZUUUP!!!

D@##!T CINDY, WHEN THEY DO IT ON THE COMMERCIAL, IT'S FUNNY. WHEN **YOU** DO IT, IT'S JUST PAINFUL!! **GOT IT**?!

HEE-HEE ... NOW YELL IT BACK AT ME!

DAG, DID YOU WRITE ALL OF THIS?!

YEP. FINALLY FINISHED THE SANTA CLAUS CONSPIRACY REPORT I STARTED LAST YEAR ...

BUT IT'S **MARCH**?! WHO'S EVEN GONNA CARE ABOUT SANTA CLAUS NOW?

NEVERTHELESS, IT IS CRITICAL INFORMATION ...

DO WE FORGET ABOUT BLACK HISTORY JUST BECAUSE IT ISN'T FEBRUARY?

YEAH. SO?

GRANNDAD, COULD YOU TAKE ME TO KINKO'S?

WHAT FOR?

I GOTTA MAKE COPIES OF MY NEWLY COMPLETED REPORT ON THE CONSPIRATORIAL LINKS BETWEEN THE ILLUMINATI AND SANTA CLAUS ... I'M THINKING I'LL DISTRIBUTE IT OVER THE INTERNET, MOSTLY ...

WHO WOULD WASTE THEIR TIME DOWNLOADING THAT NONSENSE?

... SAID THE MAN WHO SPENT FIVE HOURS TRYING TO DOWNLOAD THE "STARR REPORT."

HEY!! THAT WAS A DOCUMENT OF IMMENSE LEGAL AND POLITICAL SIGNIFICANCE!!

SORRY, MY REPORT DOESN'T HAVE ANY "FILTH-FLARN-FILTH."

41

44

We join young Michael Caesar as he comes to terms with his recent move from Brooklyn to Woodcrest, with the help of Huey and a warm beverage.

Certainly the alien environment can be a bit sobering. Even worse, he has already suffered through so much in his young life …

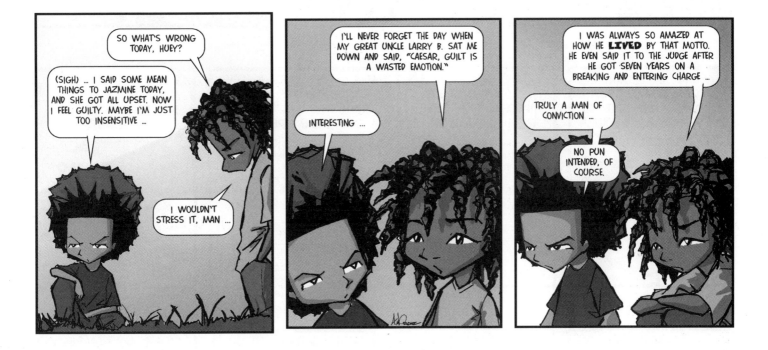

52

56

57

RILEY, YOUR BROTHER TELLS ME YOU'VE TAKEN AN INTEREST IN THE **NRA**. I FIND THIS QUITE DISCONCERTING.

I KNOW MOVIES CAN MAKE GUNS LOOK "COOL," BUT BELIEVE ME, THEY'RE DANGEROUS! I'VE FOUGHT MY WHOLE LIFE FOR MORE GUN CONTROL...

I'M ALL FOR GUN CONTROL!

REALLY? BUT I THOUGHT —

I'M GONNA USE **BOTH** HANDS! NO DOUBT!!

Thank you for your interest in the National Rifle Association. As you already know, we strive constantly to safeguard the Second Amendment freedoms of American citizens ...
The National Rifle Association is made up of hard-working American citizens just like yourself — from all walks of life and all ages.

These men and women could be your teacher, or your doctor, or your pastor. They are decent, peaceful, law-abiding citizens of this great land ...

and they have all sworn to blast the living heck out of any local, state or federal authority who attempts to restrict their constitutionally protected right to bear arms.

WOW, I THOUGHT **I** WAS HARD-CORE ...

YO HUEY, LOOK AT THIS! YOU TALK ABOUT HOW BAD THE **NRA** IS, WELL CHECK OUT WHO'S DOWN ...

IT'S THAT "MOSES" GUY FROM THAT MOVIE ...

FIRST OF ALL, MOSES ISN'T JUST A CHARACTER IN A MOVIE. SECOND, HE WASN'T WHITE. THIRD ...

I'LL CHECK THE OLD TESTAMENT, BUT I'M PRETTY SURE MOSES WASN'T PACKIN' HEAT.

WELL, IT LOOKED TO **ME** LIKE HE WAS PACKIN' MORE HEAT THAN CHARLES BRONSON, SO THERE ...

NRA, FOOL!! WHAT?!

69

OK, LET'S SEE HERE, GOT MY BAG, MY PAPERWORK ...

MY CLIPBOARD, MY BUTTON ...

WHAT ABOUT A SIDE ARM AND NIGHTSTICK? ONE OF THOSE CENSUS DODGERS MIGHT GET VIOLENT.

(SIGH) PLEASE HUSH UP, BOY.

OK BOYS, I'M OFF TO COUNT THE MASSES. HUEY, WHAT'S THE WEATHER SUPPOSED TO BE LIKE TODAY?

99?!

UMM ... PAPER SAYS THE HIGH IS GOING TO BE AROUND 99 DEGREES.

SHOOOT, THE MASSES AIN'T GOIN' NOWHERE. I'LL START TOMORROW ...

IF YOU COULD DO ANYTHING YOU WANTED TO DO WHEN YOU GREW UP, WHAT WOULD IT BE?

WELL, I GUESS IT WOULD BE TO DEDICATE MYSELF TOTALLY TO THE LIBERATION OF OPPRESSED PEOPLE AROUND THE GLOBE.

BUT YOU'RE DOING THAT NOW AND YOU'RE ALWAYS MISERABLE!

HEY, SUCCESS CAN BE ROUGH ...

BOY, WHAT ARE YOU DOING OUT HERE? DIDN'T I TELL YOU TO CUT THE GRASS?

HEY, JUST 'CAUSE I DON'T AGREE WITH WHAT YOU'RE DOING, DOESN'T MEAN I'M NOT GONNA HAVE YOUR BACK.

I DON'T NEED NO PROTECTION, BOY. I NEED MY GRASS CUT. DID YOU CUT IT?

WELL, UM, THE THING ABOUT THAT IS ...

SEE, WHAT HAD HAPPENED WAS ...

WHAT'S WRONG, BOY? YOU NEED A 'LIFELINE'?

(SIGH) GO HOME, HUEY. I DON'T NEED YOUR HELP.

LOOK, GRANDDAD. POWER IS ABOUT PERCEPTION ...

IF YOU **ACT** LIKE YOU HAVE AUTHORITY, PEOPLE WILL GIVE IT TO YOU.

BOY, I'M A CENSUS TAKER, NOT AN ATF AGENT. HOW DO I PULL THAT OFF?

I'D START BY KNOCKING WITH **THIS** — AND PUT SOME MORE BASS IN YOUR VOICE!

BOY, **PLEASE** GO HOME ...

SO PLEASE, IF YOU COULD JUST ANSWER A FEW QUESTIONS, I WOULD GREATLY —

YEAH, SURE. JUST MAKE IT QUICK — MY STORIES ARE ON.

YOU MEAN "DAYS OF OUR LOVE"? IT'S ON NOW?

YEP. YOU WANNA COME IN AND WATCH?

OOH! THEY'RE ABOUT TO NAME THE FATHER OF SHEILA'S BABY!

WELL, I THINK I CAN TAKE A SHORT BREAK ...

SO I GUESS I'LL JUST WAIT HERE, THEN, HUH?

82

SO THEY DIDN'T FIRE YOU BECAUSE I CURSED OUT THAT OLD WOMAN?

NO.

OR FOR THE EXCESSIVE FORCE, OR THE BRIBES, OR THE FACT THAT I ENUMERATED THAT ONE LADY'S JEWELRY COLLECTION ...

(SIGH) NOPE. THEY FIRED ME 'CAUSE YOU GOT TOO MUCH DONE IN ONE DAY.

SO WE'RE AGREED I'LL NEVER **EVER** HAVE TO HEAR ANOTHER LECTURE ABOUT THE VALUE OF HARD WORK, RIGHT?

BOY, I ASKED YOU TO TAKE OVER MY CENSUS ROUNDS. **YOU!** WHY DID YOU LET RILEY DO IT?

I WANTED TO HELP, REALLY. BUT A GOVERNMENT JOB GOES AGAINST MY PRINCIPLES ...

HOWEVER, I REMEMBER YOU HAD ASKED ME EARLIER TO CUT THE GRASS, SO I RUSHED HERE TO CUT IT RIGHT AWAY!

IS THAT RIGHT?

DID I MENTION I MAY BE SUFFERING FROM CLINICAL PROCRASTINATION?

HMM. YOU MAY BE SUFFERING FROM A LOT MORE THAN THAT IN A MINUTE ...

LOOK, GRANDDAD. THE TRUTH IS I THOUGHT ABOUT CUTTING THE GRASS, BUT THEN I WENT AND SAW "THE PATRIOT" INSTEAD. IT WAS TERRIBLY IRRESPONSIBLE OF ME.

YES, IT WAS!

I'M **VERY** DISAPPOINTED IN MYSELF ...

YOU SHOULD BE.

ON A TOTALLY UNRELATED NOTE, HOW WERE YOUR SOAP OPERAS?

THAT AIN'T GOT NOTHIN' TO DO WITH NOTHIN'!!!

Panel 1: (SIGH) WELL, MY LITTLE ATTEMPT AT A SUMMER JOB ENDED PRETTY AWFUL ... I'M LUCKY I **JUST** GOT FIRED ...

Panel 2: AFTER WHAT RILEY DID, THEY PROBABLY COULD HAVE ARRESTED **BOTH** OF US ... AND TO THINK THIS WHOLE THING COULD HAVE BEEN SO EASILY AVOIDED.

Panel 3: BY NOT TAKING FIVE HOURS OFF TO WATCH DAYTIME TELEVISION?

BY NEVER WORKING FOR THE SYSTEM IN THE FIRST PLACE?

BY NEVER HAVING NO **D@#N** GRANDKIDS!!

Huey Freeman's Online Movie Review
The Patriot

First, I was rather surprised that the filmmakers chose to omit Crispus Attucks from this Revolutionary War tale ...

thereby passing up a rare opportunity where they could have justifiably killed the black man first.

THAT'S STUPID ...

IT'S TRUE, THOUGH.

"The Patriot" has all the standard Hollywood cliches and historical inaccuracies about slavery that make the film easy for an intelligent black man like myself to despise.

The token black soldier who finds nobility in fighting for his oppressor, the total omission of the brutality of slavery in South Carolina during that era ... classic revisionist propaganda trash.

C'MON, MAN ... YOU GOTTA MENTION IT.

SIGH ...

But there is some intense white-on-white violence, and the cannonball decapitation was aiight. One star out of five.

Panel 1: IS THAT **SO** MUCH TO ASK? A MOVIE THAT **I** CAN RELATE TO? I CAN'T RELATE TO "**THE PATRIOT**"!

Panel 2: I WANNA SEE A MOVIE ABOUT THE **BLACK** STRUGGLE. I WANNA SEE **OUR** STORY TOLD ON THE BIG SCREEN, YOU KNOW?

SURE. YOU WANNA SEE "X-MEN."

Panel 3: EXACTLY, BUT CAN I GET JUST **ONE** MORE BLACK PERSON? **ONE**?

AND ONE **LESS** REALLY BAD WHITE WIG ... YEEESH ...

Panel 4: WELL, IT'S GOOD TO KNOW I'M NOT THE ONLY PERSON WHO ALWAYS THOUGHT THE X-MEN COMIC IS A RIP-OFF OF THE BLACK LIBERATION STRUGGLE.

OF COURSE NOT ...

Panel 5: WHILE IT'S UNKNOWN IF IT INFLUENCED STAN LEE AND JACK KIRBY WHEN THEY CREATED THE X-MEN IN 1963, OR EVEN LEN WEIN, WHO CREATED THE NEW X-MEN IN 1975, IT'S WELL KNOWN THAT AROUND THE '80S THE COMIC BOOK BEGAN TO INCREASINGLY DRAW UPON THE CIVIL RIGHTS AND BLACK POWER MOVEMENTS FOR INSPIRATION — THE PIVOTAL MOMENT OF CHANGE BEING "GOD LOVES, MAN KILLS," PUBLISHED IN 1982.

Panel 6: IT'S ALSO GOOD TO KNOW I'M NOT THE ONLY PERSON WITH A WEALTH OF WORTHLESS INFORMATION.

(SIGH) GUESS THAT'S WHY WE BOYS ...

Panel 7: SEE THAT! LEFT OUT AGAIN! **STORM** IS BARELY IN THE MOVIE AT ALL, AND WHY ARE THERE NO BLACK **MALE** X-MEN IN THE MOVIE?!

Panel 8: THEY RIP OFF OUR STRUGGLE AND ERASE US! WHAT, WE CAN'T BE MUTANTS!? THE BLACK MAN CAN **BE** A MUTANT!!

Panel 9: WELL, OF COURSE ... I MEAN, WELL ... NEVER MIND.

WHAT?

Panel 10: NOTHING. JUST STOPPING MYSELF FROM MAKING THE EASY DENNIS RODMAN JOKE.

THANK YOU, I'M TRYING TO BE SERIOUS HERE!

ARE YOU SURE A NEWSPAPER WILL REALLY REACH BLACK FOLKS? YOU ALWAYS SAY THAT AS A PEOPLE WE DON'T READ ENOUGH ...

TRUE — BUT WE'LL BE **GIVING** THE PAPER AWAY, AND BLACK FOLK'S LOVE **FREE** STUFF, SO MAYBE THEY'LL READ IT AFTER ALL.

INTERESTING ... YOU GOT A NAME FOR IT?

OH YEAH ...

"THE FREE HUEY."

TIGHT!! MAN ... USA TODAY WON'T BE ABLE TO SEE US WITH THE **HUBBLE**!

NOW THAT WE HAVE THE TITLE, WE NEED TO THINK OF A NICE TAG LINE — LIKE THE NEW YORK TIMES' "ALL THE NEWS THAT'S FIT TO PRINT."

SO FAR I'VE GOT "INFORMATION TO BREAK THE CHAINS" AND "THE SHINING BLACK LIGHT OF TRUTH."

WHICH ONE DO YOU LIKE BEST?

I DUNNO. I'M NOT REALLY FEELIN' EITHER OF THOSE.

WELL ... THERE'S ALWAYS "READ, DUMMY!"

THAT'S THE ONE!!

IT'S NOT **BAD**. IT JUST DIDN'T GRAB MY ATTENTION LIKE IT SHOULD ... I WANT YOU TO PUSH YOURSELF ...

SINCE IT'S ALREADY AN OLD STORY, WE REALLY HAVE TO DEMONSTRATE THAT OUR INTIMACY WITH THE SUBJECT MATTER SURPASSES THAT OF OUR COMPETITORS AT THE MAJOR PAPERS.

FINE. HOW 'BOUT "SEVERAL SHADY SCREWFACED SCOUNDRELS SCRAP AT SOURCE SHOW, SPECTATORS SCATTER, SNOOP SAFE!"

PERFECT.

Panel 1: HUEY FREEMAN, OWNER, PUBLISHER, EDITOR IN CHIEF AND WRITER FOR "THE FREE HUEY WORLD REPORT," BURNS THE MIDNIGHT OIL ...

SIGH ... SPORTS ...

Panel 2: HE'S RUSHING TO GET TOMORROW'S ISSUE OUT TO THE READERS WHO THIRST FOR KNOWLEDGE ...

I HATE SPORTS. I KNOW NOTHING ABOUT SPORTS.

Panel 3: REST ASSURED, HOWEVER, THAT THE RELENTLESS PURSUIT OF TRUTH IS NEVER COMPROMISED.

Tiger Woods wins everything; white folks slated to quit golf by 2004.

DONE!

Panel 4: I DON'T KNOW ... IT'S NOT A BAD EFFORT, BUT I THINK YOU TAKE TOO MANY LIBERTIES WITH THE FACTS TO CALL THIS A NEWSPAPER.

LIKE WHAT?

Panel 5: WELL, HOW DO YOU **KNOW** G.W. BUSH SMOKED CRACK?

I THINK I HEARD IT ON "THE CHRIS ROCK SHOW."

Panel 6: SO YOU PUT IT IN YOUR **NEWSPAPER**?!

C'MON, LIKE IT'S REALLY **THAT** HARD TO BELIEVE?

Panel 7: YOU'VE SEEN "BIG BROTHER." YOU WERE HOOKED ON "SURVIVOR" ... NOW **UPN** PREPARES TO TAKE REALITY SHOWS WHERE THEY'VE NEVER BEEN BEFORE ...

Panel 8: THIS FALL, WATCH 10 ORDINARY PEOPLE COMPETE FOR **TWO MILLION DOLLARS**! THE LOCATION? DETROIT. THE CHALLENGE? TO BE THE LAST ONE LEFT LIVING IN A MANSION ...

Panel 9: WITH FOUR **BIG BLACK CONVICTS**!!

SAY WHAT?

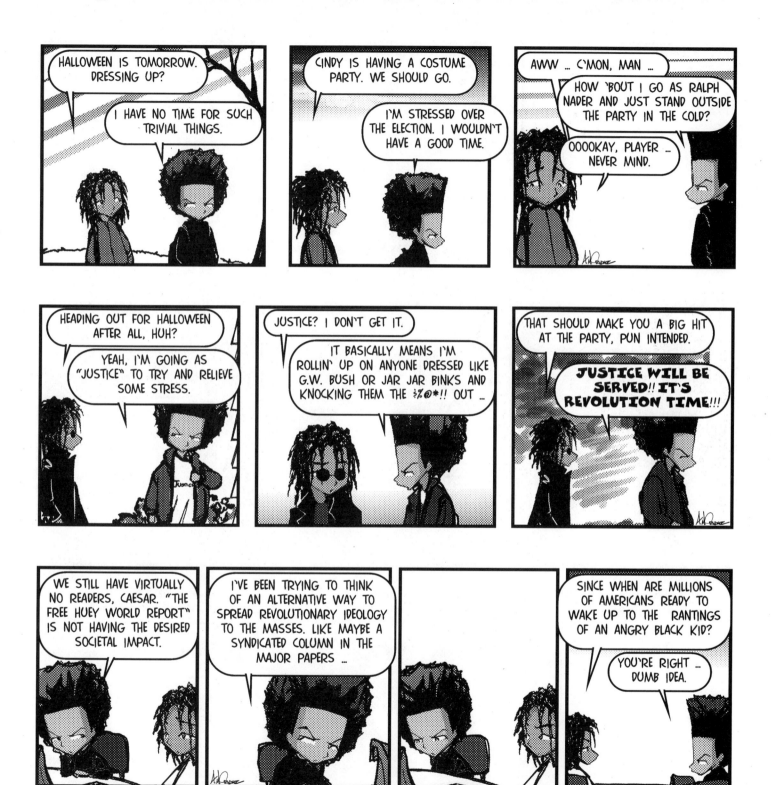